GLENN VAN EKEREN

Love
IS A VERB

10 Ways to Make All Your Relationships Great

Published by SimpleTruths, LLC
1952 McDowell Road, Suite 300
Naperville, Illinois 60563

Design: Lynn Harker, Simple Truths, Illinois
Edited by: Alice Patenaude

Simple Truths is a registered trademark.
Printed and bound in the United States of America

ISBN 978-1-60810-244-0

800-900-3427
www.simpletruths.com

01 WOZ 13

Acknowledgments

My heartfelt thanks to the following people:
My wife, Marty, for her continual encouragement,
friendship, and willingness to stick with me through
thick and thin. To my children, Matt and Katy, for
believing in their dad and allowing me to tell stories
about them. To all my friends and family who encouraged me to turn my writing dreams into reality.

Table of Contents

Introduction

I felt an emotional tug on my heart several times during the 2009 movie release of *The Blind Side*. This semi-biographical movie beautifully portrayed the life-changing power of love.

For most of his childhood, 17-year-old Michael Oher lived in one foster care home after another, due to his mother's drug addiction. That is until Leigh Anne Tuohy came into his life. She noticed Michael walking on the road, shivering in the cold. When she learns he intended to spend the night huddled outside the school gym, she offered him a place to stay.

Michael's life was never the same. The Tuohy family accepted him, believed in Michael, encouraged him, challenged him to improve his academic performance and ultimately nurtured his athletic ability; paving the way for Michael to become an NFL star.

The Tuohy family was a living, breathing example that **Love is a Verb**.

So many books, manuals and seminars have been written about love. As a matter of fact, the Bible talks about love from the first book to the last book. Think of the multitude of poems, songs and letters that are inspired by love. It might seem like the topic has been exhausted. Considering all the advice we've received, love should be naturally expressed to sustain and nurture harmonious, cooperative and mutually beneficial relationships.

Unfortunately, we haven't necessarily reached that point. Maybe we read but don't respond, listen but don't understand, or know what to do but fail to take action. Whatever the case, relationships are in constant need of a practical injection of love.

There is a constant pull between what we want our relationships to be and what they are. **Love is a Verb** is about those simple, yet often forgotten, accumulations of little actions that contribute to building our relationships into what we want them to become.

I sincerely desire to be a positive influence in people's lives, to become what I often call a picker-upper-person. These people are masters at building and maintaining quality relationships. They understand the dynamics for improving their casual and most intimate interactions. To them, **Love is a Verb**, and genuinely caring for others is a way of life. Picker-upper-people transform lives and relationships by activating the qualities of a people builder.

Choose any selection in this book and discover an insightful comment, powerful illustration, or practical strategy that will help you:

- ❤ Accept people for who they are

- ❤ Identify what people need to feel good about themselves

- ❤ Make your relationships bloom

- ❤ Get along with difficult people

- ❤ Effectively deal with conflict

- ❤ Develop a sincere interest in others

- ❤ Build on people's positive qualities

- ❤ Forgive hurtful actions

- ❤ Help others feel encouraged, uplifted and motivated to become all they can be

- ❤ Be the type of person people enjoy being around

This book is all about making a positive difference in people's lives. It is packed with timeless wisdom, proven principles, simple actions, and contemporary insight that will help you create increased enjoyment in your relationships. You'll be inspired to rekindle the warmth in your friendships, marriage and work relationships.

One final thing. There is a side benefit to **Love is a Verb**. People who *act* as though love is a verb often find that others treat them the same way. It's funny how life tends to give back what we give. One thing is for sure, those you touch will not remain as they are—and I doubt you will either.

Glenn Van Ekeren

"Love is our true destiny.
We do not find the meaning of life by
ourselves alone—we find it with another."

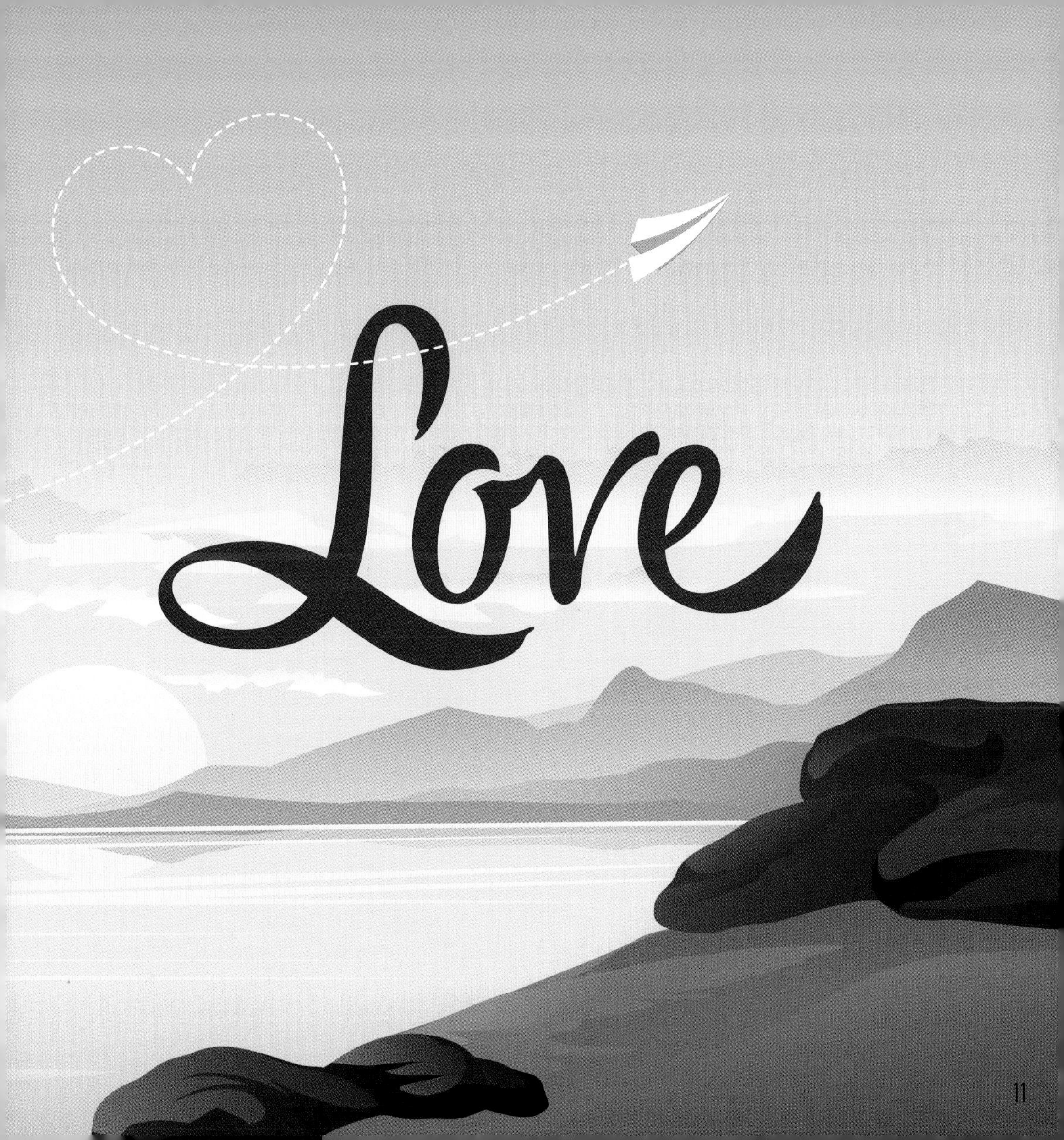
Love

Good Advice—
Wrong Application

> *"There is little doubt that most of us long for stronger, more creative and rewarding ways of loving each other."*
>
> *Leo F. Buscaglia*

Constant conflict caused an engaged couple to question their wedding plans. The man, concerned he could lose the woman he loved, realized he had no idea how to handle many unresolved issues. So, he sought the advice of a counselor who suggested the problems could be solved if he would take up biking. "I want you to ride ten miles a day for the next two weeks and then check back with me."

Two weeks later the man reported back to his counselor as requested. "So, how are you and your fiancée doing now?" the counselor inquired.

"How should I know," the man replied, "I'm one hundred forty miles away from home, and I haven't talked to her for fourteen days."

There will always be challenges and problems in relationships. No problem! Dr. Theodore Rubin advises in *One to One*: "The problem is not that there are problems. The problem is expecting otherwise and thinking that having problems is a problem."

Abundant advice is available from assorted sources for anyone wishing to enrich their relationships. Unfortunately, none of that advice works unless you're willing to step up your investment in people.

If you remember the following, your relationships will never be the same.

1. Creating and nourishing relationships is hard work.

2. There will always be problems.

3. Relationships are worth every ounce of effort it takes to work through the unavoidable challenges.

This is good advice, if I must say so myself. Apply it now.

"I like long walks,
especially when they
are taken by people
who annoy me."

FRED ALLEN

Making acts
of Love

no matter how we feel

> "Happy marriages begin
> when we marry the ones we love,
> and they blossom when we love
> the ones we marry."
>
> *Tom Mullen*

Dr. Joyce Brothers tells the story of a judge trying to change the mind of a woman filing for divorce. "You're 92," he said. "Your husband is 94. You've been married for 73 years. Why give up now?"

"Our marriage has been on the rocks for quite a while," the woman explained, "but we decided to wait until the children died."

Dr. Robert Taylor, co-author of *Couples—The Art of Staying Together*, said, "We're now living in the age of disposability: Use it once, and throw it away. Over the past decade, there has developed a feeling that relationships are equally disposable."

The throwaway culture in which we live seems intent on throwing out the principle that marriage is a commitment requiring effort.

A *U.S. News & World Report* study reveals the biggest reason couples split up. It is the "inability to talk honestly with each other, to bare their souls, and to treat each other as their best friend."

Maybe you are familiar with this type of scenario. Your spouse complains, "You never tell me you love me anymore." Taking the hint, you mumble, "Of course I love you." You say that while thinking, "Silly, I wouldn't be living with you if I didn't love you. If anything ever changes, you'll be the first to know." Why don't we just respond with a warm kiss and say, "I'm sorry I haven't told you lately how much I love you?"

The great psychologist, Dr. George W. Crane, said in his famous book *Psychology Applied:* "Remember, motions are the precursors of emotions. You can't control the latter directly but only through your choice of motions or actions…To avoid this all too common tragedy (marital difficulties and misunderstandings) become aware of the true psychological facts. Go through the proper motions each day and you'll soon begin to feel the corresponding emotions! Just be sure you and your mate go through those motions of dates and kisses, the phrasing of sincere daily compliments, plus the many other little courtesies and you need not worry about the emotion of love. You can't act devoted for very long without feeling devoted."

When you treat your spouse as the most important person in your life, you will begin feeling it, believing it, and enjoying it. What can you do this week to turn acts into love no matter what your emotions are telling you?

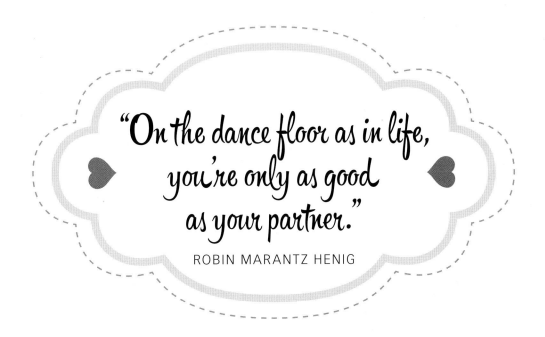

"On the dance floor as in life, you're only as good as your partner."

ROBIN MARANTZ HENIG

"The greatest gift that you can give
to others is the gift of unconditional
love and acceptance."

BRIAN TRACY

Acceptance

My Wife

Is Always Right

> "If you are losing a tug-of-war
> with a tiger, give him the rope
> before he gets to your arm.
> You can always buy a new rope."
>
> *Max Gunther*

My wife, Marty, rarely calls me at work. She's made it a habit not to interrupt my day unless there's an emergency or an issue needing immediate attention. As a result, I was a bit anxious returning her call when I returned from a meeting to see a note stating I should call her as soon as possible.

"Hello, sweetheart," I said. "What's up?"

"A bad thing happened," she sheepishly replied. "You know, it's really noisy when you back your car into the garage door."

"Pardon me," I responded, attempting to visualize the scene.

"It's your fault," she continued. "When you left for work this morning, you left your garage door open. I entered the detached garage through your open door and the garage was so well lit from the outside light I didn't realize my door was closed."

"It's my fault?" I chuckled.

"Yes, and now the door is shattered."

Marty and I have laughed about that situation many times. I, of course, continue to remind her that I was not the one in the driver's seat. However, I learned a few important things about potential conflicts, arguments, and marital disputes from this unfortunate incident. First, scratched bumpers and dented trunks can be fixed. They are not worth getting upset about, especially at the expense of harmony.

Secondly, and this is most important, I learned my wife is always right. Now don't get me wrong here. I don't mean to say that I am always wrong, but I carefully choose the issues worth debating. I often recall the advice of Jonathan Kozol: *"Pick battles big enough to matter, small enough to win."* In other words, decide what issues are worth dying for and which ones you refuse to argue about.

Newspaper and magazine editor H. L. Mencken often drew letters of criticism and outrage from his critiques of American life. He answered every critical letter and handled each one the same way. Mencken simply wrote back, "You may be right." What a marvelous way to diffuse a potentially volatile situation.

For most of us, the hardest thing to give is the "giving in." Wanting to win fuels the fire. It causes arguments to digress into lose-lose situations. Maybe that's why Ben Franklin believed, "If you argue and rankle and contradict, you may achieve a victory sometimes; but it will be an empty victory because you will never get your opponent's good will."

Franklin's comment reminds me of the couple traveling down the highway in complete silence. An earlier argument left both unwilling to concede their positions. Passing a barnyard of mules, the husband sarcastically asked, "Are they relatives of yours?"

"Yes," his wife replied. "I married into the family." Ouch!

Sydney J. Harris submitted, "The most important thing in an argument, next to being right, is to leave an escape hatch for your opponent, so that he can gracefully swing over to your side without too much apparent loss of face." That's why I've adopted the attitude that my wife (and any other potential opponent) is always right, even though in the long run my conviction might be proven right.

What's the benefit of taking such an approach? Isn't this escaping, avoiding, and choosing the easy way out? I suppose you could look at it like that. Even though I know there are two sides to every issue— my side, and the side that no informed, intelligent, clear-thinking, self-respecting person could possibly hold (only kidding)—any quarrel will not last long if we refuse to continue stirring it up by trying to prove others wrong.

Two men, Jake and Sam, were stuck together on a deserted island. They got along so well that not one cross word passed between them. In fact, their passive behavior made life so harmonious that it became monotonous at times.

One day Jake came up with an idea to break the boredom. "Let's have a heated argument," he suggested, "like people back home often have." Sam responded, "But we don't have anything to argue about." Jake thought for a moment and then suggested, "Let's find a bottle that's washed up on shore and place it on the beach between us. I'll say, 'This bottle is mine!' And you'll say, 'No, it isn't. The bottle is mine!' That will surely get a good argument started."

So, finding a bottle and placing it on the sandy beach between them, Jake exclaimed, "This bottle is mine!" Sam, pausing for moment, responded meekly, "I think, my friend, that the bottle is mine." "Oh, really?" Jake said agreeably. "If the bottle is yours, take it."

It is not humanly possible to carry on an argument between two people when one refuses to argue. So, here's a thought: Let people be right until the heat has subsided and you can discuss the situation rationally.

Two months after our car crashed into the garage door and we had purchased a minivan with a luggage carrier (don't get ahead of me), I got another call at work. "Glenn, you closed your door, but my garage door didn't go up high enough. The luggage carrier hooked the garage door and shattered it. The luggage carrier isn't in great shape either."

You can draw your own conclusions about how this conversation ended.

A married couple was involved in another round of repeated disagreements. The same issue had been bitterly discussed over and over. The wife finally blurted in desperation, *"You're impossible!"*

Not missing a beat, the husband retorted, *"No, I'm next to impossible."*

Creating a Relationship
Masterpiece

> *"A relationship is a living thing. It needs and benefits from the same attention to detail that an artist lavishes on his art."*
>
> *David Viscott*

That's a nice quote from David Viscott, isn't it? Let's carry his artistic thought a bit further, though. Consider the following qualities present in relationship masterpieces.

- Start with a blank canvas of acceptance. Permit people to be who they are—not what they could be, should be, or would be if only they listened to you. Accept the imperfections. Celebrate each person's individuality. Acceptance affirms peoples' value, raises self-esteem, and makes them feel comfortable in your presence.

- Artists are masters at the use of primary colors, which create the heart of the finished product. Mutual trust is one such primary ingredient. We live in an imperfect, messy world made up of imperfect people. Unfortunately, many of us are prone to trusting people only when they prove themselves trustworthy. I tend to believe that if we trust people, they will prove themselves trustworthy. I know that trust can be betrayed, but trust is essential for relationships to develop. Step out. Make an effort to believe in the intrinsic goodness of people. Sure, you might be disappointed, but you will also be blessed.

- Sharing yourself with others is a scary risk. Withholding who we are places a permanent blemish on the relationship canvas. Honest communication stands out in any close friendship. Use discretion, but share your hurts, fears and failures. Throw in the good stuff with the bad stuff. Just refrain from unnecessary critical, cheap-shot, or hurting comments that are better left unsaid.

I'm sure every artist has a favorite color that tends to find its way into each creation. My favorite relationship ingredient is improving the ability to see the good in people. Tell your friends, family and coworkers what you like about them. Tell people how thankful you are for them. Recognize their talents, applaud their successes (one of the most difficult actions of human nature), and make others feel important about themselves. Expressing appreciation on every possible occasion is one of the surest ways to boost mutual respect and encourage positive behaviors.

A masterpiece stands out in the viewer's mind when the proper highlights are added. When it comes to relationships, you can move to the next level by:

- Giving more than you get
- Allowing people to have their space
- Maintaining confidentiality
- Giving supportive and positive advice
- Being loyal
- Listening

- Treating others with dignity
- Saying "please" and "thank you"
- Being agreeable
- Accepting others' opinions
- Forgiving wrongs committed

Quality relationships are fulfilling. Relationships don't fail to become beautiful experiences because they are wrong, but because most people don't want to invest what it takes to create an original. To evaluate how effective you are in creating a relationship masterpiece, just ask yourself,

> "If I were my friend,
> would I enjoy the artistic strokes (qualities)
> I experience being with me?"

"I am loyal in relationships.
Any relationship. When I go out with
my mom I don't look at other moms and say,
'Oooh, I wonder what her macaroni
and cheese tastes like.'"

GARY SHANDLING

SECTION THREE

"When you forgive, you in no way
change the past—but you sure
do change the future."

BERNARD MELTZER

Forgiveness

Placing People in
Proper Perspective

> "The primary joy of life is the acceptance, approval, sense of appreciation and companionship of our human comrades. Many men do not understand that the need for fellowship is really as deep as the need for food, and so they go throughout life accepting many substitutes for genuine, warm, simple relatedness."
>
> —*Joshua Loth Liebman*

Barbara Bush was not Wellesley College's first choice as their 1990 graduation commencement speaker. Some of the seniors didn't view her as a role model for the issues facing today's modern woman.

"To honor Barbara Bush as a commencement speaker," they protested, "is to honor a woman who has gained recognition through the achievements of her husband, which contradicts what we have been taught the past four years."

The First Lady handled the accusations in her classy style; she didn't allow the protests to offend or intimidate her. Mrs. Bush spoke from her heart about the fulfillment she had experienced from her traditional values. She offered this advice in her commencement address:

"Cherish your human connections, your relationships with friends and family. For several years, you've had impressed upon you the importance to your career of dedication and hard work. This is true, but as important as your obligations as a doctor, lawyer, or business leader will be, you are a human being first, and those human con-nections—with spouses, with children, with friends—are the most important investments you will ever make. At the end of your life, you will never regret not having passed one more test, not winning one more verdict, or not closing one more deal. You will regret time not spent with a husband, a friend, a child or a parent."

The First Lady addressed the heart of living. All of our personal and professional endeavors are made sweeter, richer, and more satisfy-ing by sharing them with others. As Antoine de Saint-Exupery wrote, "There is no hope of joy except in human relationships."

Too often, what should matter most in our lives receives the least attention. Battles with the almighty dollar, pursuing selfish interests, attaining that next promotion, or closing a deal are empty pursuits without the human element. It's easy to forget that our relationships are what encourage the heart and nourish the soul. Harold Kushner, in *When All You've Ever Wanted Isn't Enough*, wrote: "A life without people, without the same people day after day, people who belong to us, people who will be there for us, people who need us and whom we need in return, may be very rich in other things, but in human terms, it is no life at all."

A life without relationships limits the value of everything we do. Regardless of the pressures you feel to succeed in our "what's-in-it-for-me" society, don't make the mistake of placing value on only those activities and goals that enhance your paycheck. Maintain the proper perspective of people. You will never regret it.

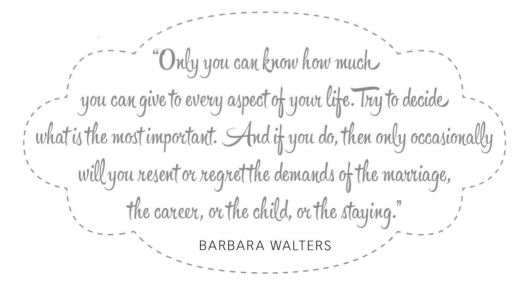

"Only you can know how much you can give to every aspect of your life. Try to decide what is the most important. And if you do, then only occasionally will you resent or regret the demands of the marriage, the career, or the child, or the staying."

BARBARA WALTERS

Be Willing to Say "I'm Sorry"

> "…The most deadly of all sins
> is the mutilation of a child's spirit."
>
> *Erik H. Erikson*

I cherish so much about our children. Through my many years of parenting, this is what I treasure the most: each relationship.

Oh, I admit it's nice when they scored points in a basketball game or gracefully performed a dance routine. I was pleased when their report cards revealed above-average scores, or when I observed the effort put into a school project. And of course it was flattering when people commented about how nice they looked or how respectful they were.

But what really tripped my trigger and renewed my parental energy—after returning from a speaking trip, or working on a free throw shot, playing taxi driver, or setting curfew—was a loving smile, a hug, a high five, and the four cherished words: "I love you, Dad."

I'm keenly aware how my actions, words, tone of voice, or nonverbals affected the loving, caring, and mutually respectful relationship we enjoy. And, I've failed at times, as a father, to uphold my end of the responsibility. There have been situations when I crushed my children's spirits.

When my son was in the sixth grade, another dad and I agreed to coach a traveling basketball team. Along with our two sons, we invited ten other boys to enjoy the experience with us.

It didn't take long for me to realize that the definition of a father-coach is someone who expects his son to be everything he wasn't. I upheld high and sometimes unrealistic expectations. I even found it easy to justify my demands by attempting to motivate my son to be the best he could be. However, during one game I overstepped my parental privileges.

The game was already won. The boys fought courageously to overcome a major point deficit to hold a comfortable lead with thirty-seven seconds left in the game. Out of nowhere Matt (my son) stole the ball, dribbled the length of the court, and *missed* an uncontested lay-up.

I chose to release my accumulated tension from the game on my son for missing that lay-up. The shot meant nothing. We had won the game and advanced to the finals. Matt played with heart and gave his all, yet he blew that simple lay-up. I let him know in no uncertain terms how disappointed I was and how ridiculous it was for him to miss such a simple shot.

The joy of winning drained from his face. He stood motionless and speechless as Dad continued to drain the power from his self-esteem battery. I knew I'd blown it, but I continued to justify my outburst and dug myself into a deeper hole.

The next hours waiting for the championship game were long and quiet. Matt was hurting inside, and I was full of guilt. There was little question that I needed my son's forgiveness.

Sitting in our van outside the gymnasium, I slowly turned to look into Matt's fearful and discouraged face. "Matt, I was wrong," I began. "I'm sorry for blowing up at you. You worked hard in that game and I failed to recognize you for all the good things you did. Please forgive me."

It was then that Matt touched my heart, and my eyes filled with tears. "It's okay, Dad. I know you love me."

Thanks to my son, I could walk into the championship game with a clear conscience, a repaired heart, and a softer spirit.

We lost the championship game by one point, but I came out of that tournament a winner. My son had forgiven me.

The only way to heal a damaged spirit is to swallow the parental pride and say, "I'm sorry. I was wrong. Please forgive me." Failure to bring healing when you've been unfair or hurtful can breed anger for years to come.

When was the last time you told your child, "I'm sorry for anything I have ever said or done that has hurt you"?

"If you were to ask what is the hardest task in the world, you might think of some muscular feat, some acrobatic challenge, some chore to be done on the battlefield or the playing field. Actually, however, there is nothing which we find more arduous than saying, 'I was wrong.'"

SUNSHINE MAGAZINE

"You cannot do a kindness too soon,
for you never know how soon
it will be too late."

RALPH WALDO EMERSON

Kindness

Don't Overlook Little
Acts of Kindness

> "At the hour of death, when we come face to face with God, we are going to be judged on love—not how much we have done, but how much love we put into our actions."
>
> *Mother Teresa*

Mr. and Mrs. Dwight Morrow, together with their daughter, Anne [future wife of Charles Lindbergh], called on Governor [Calvin] Coolidge at the Hotel Touraine, in Boston. On the train ride back to New York, several people came into their drawing-room, and Coolidge's name was introduced. Morrow said that Coolidge had Presidential possibilities, but several men disagreed, and one broke out, "No one would like him." Then Anne [age six] spoke up, holding out a finger bound with adhesive tape, "*I* like him. He was the only one that asked about my sore finger." Morrow looked pleased and said, "There's your answer."

Anne had a good point. Maybe asking a little girl about her sore finger isn't necessarily a bona fide qualification for the presidency, but a spirit of kindness is a surefire way to impress others. Kindness, the sincere expression of love, makes the people around you feel loved and valuable.

English author Rita Snowden reflected on a visit she made to a village not far from Dover. She vividly recalled how, as she sat drinking tea at a sidewalk cafe in the afternoon sun of a balmy spring day, she suddenly became aware of a pleasant smell that filled the air.

She said it was as though she was suddenly surrounded by flowers. When Snowden asked where the pleasant aroma was coming from, she was told that it was from the people who worked in a nearby perfume factory. Most of the village's residents worked in a perfume factory in the middle of town. At 4:30, when the workday was over, their clothing was saturated with the perfume scent that accompanied them as they entered the streets.

Opportunities to show kindness abound. If someone were to pay you ten cents for every kindness you ever showed and collect five cents for every unkind word or action, would you be rich or poor?

Flash a smile to those you meet on the street. William Arthur Ward believed, "A warm smile is the universal language of kindness."

Use the precious words *please* and **thank you** at every possible occasion. St. Ambrose suggested that, "No duty is more urgent than that of returning thanks."

Show concern for those inflicted with little hurts and big ones. Allow others to go in front of you in the grocery line (that's a tough one for me). Make it possible for people to change lanes in heavy traffic. Open the door for someone entering the same building as you. Offer a warm greeting to people you meet walking in hotel hallways.

You might be thinking, "Isn't this a bit simplistic?" You're right. But remember what impressed young Anne Morrow. It was a sensitive expression of concern for a bandaged finger that made a positive impression. Simple? Maybe. Effective? No doubt. It's the consistency of our little acts of kindness that cause people to smell a pleasant aroma about us wherever we go.

❤ *"Spread your love everywhere you go,"*

encouraged Mother Teresa. *"First of all in your own house. Give love to your children, to your wife or husband, to a next door neighbor ... Let no one ever come to you without leaving better and happier. Be the living expression of God's kindness; kindness in your face, kindness in your eyes, kindness in your smile, kindness in your warm greeting."*

"When we remember our unkindness to friends who have passed beyond the veil, we wish we could have them back again, if only for a moment, so that we could go on our knees to them and say, 'Have pity and forgive.'"

MARK TWAIN

Kindness

as a Lifestyle

> "Never lose sight of the fact that the most important yardstick of your success will be how you treat other people—your family, friends, and coworkers, and even strangers you meet along the way."
>
> *Barbara Bush*

I read a story about a woman who answered the knock on her door to find a man with a sad expression.

"I'm sorry to disturb you," he said, "but I'm collecting money for an unfortunate family in the neighborhood. The husband is out of work, the kids are hungry, the shelves are bare, the utilities will soon be cut off, and worse, they're going to be kicked out of their apartment if they don't pay the rent by this afternoon."

"I'd be happy to help out," said the woman with great concern.

"But who are you?"

"I'm the landlord," he replied.

Suffice it to say the landlord was not an enviable example of kindness. At the same time we can probably all relate to times when kindness was used to get our own way or to convince someone to do something that would benefit us. But pure kindness flows from pure motives.

Chuck Wall, a human relations instructor at Bakersfield College in California, was watching a local news program one day when a cliché from a broadcaster caught his attention: "Another random act of senseless violence."

Wall had an idea. He gave an unusual and challenging assignment to his students. They were to do something out of the ordinary to help someone. They were to then write an essay about it.

Wall then dreamed up a bumper sticker that read, "Today, I will commit one random act of senseless KINDNESS . . . will you?" Students sold the bumper stickers for one dollar each and donated the profits to a county Braille center.

An impressive variety of acts of kindness were performed. One student paid his mother's utility bills. Another student bought thirty blankets from the Salvation Army and took them to homeless people gathered under a bridge.

The idea expanded. Bumper stickers were slapped on all one hundred thirteen county patrol cars. The message was trumpeted from pulpits, in schools, and endorsed by professional associations.

As Chuck Wall reflected on the success of his idea, he commented, "I had no idea our community was in such need of something positive."

It's not just your community, Mr. Wall, that needs random acts of kindness.

After Wausau, Wisconsin was featured as the subject of a negative story on *60 Minutes*, the *Wausau Daily Herald* talked area businesses into co-sponsoring a "Random Acts of Kindness Week."

Businesses, organizations, and individuals were encouraged to perform simple acts of kindness for people they knew or didn't know. The response was gigantic. Over two hundred businesses and organizations participated. The employees of the newspaper wore "Random Acts of Kindness" T-shirts and performed good deeds.

Banks washed car windows in the drive-up lanes. Church groups mowed lawns for people in the neighborhood. Movie theaters gave out free passes to people waiting in line. One individual walked into a restaurant and bought a cup of coffee for every person in the place. The newspaper ran a hotline for people to phone in the acts of kindness they had witnessed. More than five hundred calls were received. The response was so tremendous that the *Wausau Daily Herald* decided to repeat the event the next year.

This week, how about creating a random-acts-of-kindness lifestyle? Our motto would be, "Every day, in some way, I will show kindness to someone who is not in a position to repay me." We might be amazed at how the idea grows.

> *Our motto would be, "Every day, in some way, I will show kindness to someone who is not in a position to repay me."*

"Courtesy is the one coin
you can never have too much
of or be stingy with."

John Wanamaker

"A friend is one who
knows you and loves
you just the same."

ELBERT HUBBARD

Portrait of a
Friendship

> "A friend is someone we can count on
> for understanding, support, discretions,
> and, if we're lucky, insight, wisdom,
> and well-timed foolishness."
>
> —*John R. O'Neil*

Reflect on the following view of friendship from the *Book of Sunshine.* Those who turn their radio dials to sports commentaries will perhaps have relished this human interest story of President Dwight Eisenhower.

It occurred in a little town in Kansas, where Dwight Eisenhower spent his boyhood days. He was a comely lad, strong and virile, filled with the spirit of an athlete. He chose boxing as his pastime, and his ambition and skilled technique soon made him the champion boxer of the town. There was none who dared challenge young Eisenhower's prowess.

But one day, there came to town another young man. He gave his name as Frankie Brown. Brown bore the reputation of a professional boxer, and he soon learned of the ambitious young Eisen-

hower. A match was arranged between the two young athletes. No one was ever able to tell who won the honors, but both fought so well that before the bout was over, the two were fast friends.

They retired to a restaurant following the affair, and there they discussed plans for their future. Eisenhower desired to go to college, but Brown wanted to pursue boxing as a professional career. Eisenhower sought to persuade Brown first to acquire the higher schooling. In the wee hours of the night, the two emerged, both determined to go to college.

Frankie Brown entered Notre Dame—as Knute Kenneth Rockne. The determination that led him to follow Dwight Eisenhower's advice also stood him in good stead, in becoming the noted and beloved football coach of Notre Dame.

In a fateful hour on March 31, 1931, the airplane in which Knute Rockne traveled to see his old friend in Kansas crashed to earth, crushing a life that had matched the determination, friendship, and prowess of an Eisenhower.

Once, while sitting in a restaurant, the late Henry Ford was asked: "Who is your best friend?"

Ford thought for a moment, then took out his pencil and wrote in large letters on the tablecloth: "My best friend is the one who brings out the best in me."

Rockne and Eisenhower's friendship exemplified this belief. They challenged each other, encouraged each other to raise the bar on their personal expectations, and built a relationship around mutual respect. That combination inspired Knute Rockne and Dwight Eisenhower to reach for their potential.

It's enjoyable to have friends who make us laugh. I cherish friends who offer sincere advice. Friends who want to understand what's important to me are so valuable. I respect friends who genuinely celebrate my successes and encourage me through my failures. I don't want to leave out friends who help me maintain my child-like, fun spirit, but the friend who challenges me to be all God intended can't be replaced. Everybody needs a friend like that.

"The easiest kind of relationship
for me is with ten thousand people.
The hardest is with one."
JOAN BAEZ

Are You Filling People Up
or Sucking Them Dry?

> "To do something, however small, to make others happier and better is the highest ambition, the most elevating hope, which can inspire a human being."
>
> *John Lubbock*

Success and fulfillment in life are in direct proportion to the investment we make in people. If someone spent the whole day with you, how would they feel at the end of the day—filled up or sucked dry? Are you the kind of person who searches for ways to inject hope, encouragement, and goodwill into others, or do you extract those necessities from others in your daily interaction?

The good news is that no one needs to live a minute longer extracting life out of people. We can all increase our building, filling and replenishing habits. By doing so, we make it possible for people to like themselves and their lives better when they are with us.

You want that, don't you? Not sure how? Consider the following practical actions to put on your daily relationship agenda.

Remember the basics. In 1860, the Lady Elgin collided with a lumber barge on a stormy night and sank, leaving 393 people stranded in the waters of Lake Michigan. Two hundred seventy-nine of these people drowned. A young college student named Edward Spencer plunged into the water again and again to rescue people. After he had pulled seventeen people from the freezing water, he was overcome with exhaustion and collapsed, never to stand again. For the remainder of his life, Spencer was confined to a wheelchair. Some years later, it was noted that not one of the seventeen persons he saved ever came to thank him.

How could seventeen, who had their lives spared by this young man, fail to show their gratitude? Before we judge them too harshly, it might be worth our time to evaluate our consistency in remembering life's basic manners. Smile. Say "please" and "thank you." Use people's first names when visiting with them. Greet people with a hearty "hello" or "good morning." Show interest in your coworkers' welfare. Maintain a positive, optimistic outlook on matters many people tend to frown at. Think about how others feel. Be an advocate of dignity and respect for all people.

The value of these basics is too often overlooked, taken for granted or missed completely. These simple actions communicate the caring and compassionate attitudes that encouragers possess. Review the list again. Find ways to frequently do the little acts of kindness that produce big dividends.

Honk an encouraging message. Have you ever noticed how some friendships, marriages, and parent-child relationships are vibrant and growing while others seem to be plagued with discouragement? It may be a difference in attitude. If people build up and encourage one another, the whole atmosphere is refreshing. But critical, negative spirits breed tension and conflict.

Bruce Larson, in his book *Wind & Fire*, illustrates the power of en-couragement. Writing about sand hill cranes, he wrote, "These large birds, who fly great distances across continents, have three remark-able qualities. First, they rotate leadership. No one bird stays out in front all the time. Second, they choose leaders who can handle turbulence. And then [this is my favorite], all during the time one bird is leading, the rest are honking their affirmation."

Conduct an attitude check. Are you critical of people, situations and life in general? Do you complain about the job someone else is doing or should have done? Do you have a negative spirit? If so, work to become a positive "honking" friend, spouse, parent or coworker. Negative sourpusses are energy suckers. Positive horn honkers inspire others to fly farther and higher.

Isn't it amazing how the unique habits of a sand hill crane are applicable to us? When people consistently build up and encourage, the whole atmosphere of their relationships is nurturing. People feel safe. They are comfortable taking risks. They experience healthier feelings about themselves. Virginia Arcastle said, "When people are made to feel secure, important, and appreciated, it will no longer be necessary for them to whittle down others in order to seem bigger in comparison."

Check your interactions. What kind of messages have you been honking lately? Any affirmation?

Believe in people. Dale Carnegie said, "Tell your child, your husband, or your employee that he or she is stupid or dumb at a certain thing, has no gift for it, and is doing it all wrong, and you have destroyed almost every incentive to try to improve. But use the opposite technique—be liberal with your encouragement; make the thing seem easy to do, let the other person know that you have faith in his ability to do it, that he has an undeveloped flair for it—and he will practice until the dawn comes in the window in order to excel."

According to a selection in the March 1992 *Homemade*, a young man in London wanted to be a writer, but the cards seemed stacked against him. He had only four years of school, and his father was in jail because he couldn't pay his debts. Just to survive the pain of hunger, he got a job pasting labels on bottles in a rat-infested warehouse. He slept in an attic with two other boys from the slums. With such little confidence in himself and in his ability to write, he secretly slipped out in the middle of the night to mail his first manuscript so nobody would laugh at his dream. That manuscript, along with countless others, was rejected. Finally, one story was accepted. He wasn't paid anything, but the editor praised him for his writing. That one little compliment caused him to wander aimlessly through the streets with tears rolling down his cheeks. The compliment inspired him to continue and improve. It also led to a brilliant career for Charles Dickens.

Donald Laird said, "Always help people increase their own self-esteem. Develop your skill in making other people feel important. There is hardly a higher compliment you can pay an individual than helping him be useful and to find satisfaction from his usefulness."

Expressing your belief and faith in people can provide the inspiration for someone to pursue their dreams. Find the seed of achievement waiting for your nourishment. Help people believe in themselves more than they believe in themselves, and watch them blossom.

Express your love. I fear too many of us might be represented by the guy who exclaimed to his wife, "Honey, when I think about how much I love you, I can hardly keep from telling you."

Telling someone how much they mean to you seems like a basic relationship action—and it should be. But it's not. We may want to tell others how much they mean to us, but we don't. We want to hear words of love and affection and are disappointed at how infrequently those messages touch our ears. By our very nature, our hearts respond to a message of love.

In his book *In the Arena*, former President Richard Nixon reflected on the depression he experienced following his resignation from the presidency and then undergoing surgery. At the depths of his discouragement, he told his wife, Pat, that he just wanted to die.

At Mr. Nixon's lowest point, a nurse entered the room, pulled open the drapes, and pointed to a small airplane flying back and forth. The plane was pulling a banner which read: God Loves You, And So Do We. Ruth Graham, evangelist Billy Graham's wife, had arranged for the plane to fly by the hospital. That's when Nixon experienced a turning point. Seeing that expression of love gave him the courage and desire to keep going and recover.

Somebody once said, "Appreciating others without telling them is like winking at someone in the dark; you know what you're doing, but nobody else does."

Don't just think about expressing your love and appreciation for those you care about. Take the initiative. Don't wait for the other person; the two of you could wait a long time. Never assume people know how you feel about them. Give someone close to you a hug, pat them on the back, and say, "I love you," or "You mean a lot to me," or "I care about you."

It feels good.

Someone might say, "I'm not into this 'touchy-feely' stuff. I'm uncomfortable giving hugs or verbal praise." If you are saying amen to that, here's another option: write a letter or send a note to brighten someone's day. Who could benefit from a note of appreciation, a word of concern, or a card complimenting them for a job well done? Don't let the impulse slip by without taking action. Tread yourself a well-worn path to the mailbox.

Uphold people's self-esteem. I like Henry Ward Beecher's observation that, "There are persons so radiant, so genial, so kind, so pleasure-bearing, that you instinctively feel good in their presence that they do you good, whose coming into a room is like bringing a lamp there."

I had the privilege of working several years as a volunteer with junior high youth in a basketball program. It would be self-gratifying to say I was always the type of person Beecher described, but I wasn't. I did learn, however, that when I built up a young person's self-esteem, they were open to instruction.

Imagine twelve-year-old Laurie struggling to get the little round ball through the round cylinder. She's zero for ten, and you approach her saying, "Laurie, I like the way you put everything into your shot. I think you're going to make a good basketball player."

Laurie beams. She is receptive and eager to learn more. Laurie is all ears when you add, "Laurie, you tend to throw your elbow out and shoot off your palms. Let me show you the proper shooting method."

Sounds simple, doesn't it? The beauty is that upholding a person's self-esteem is simple if our motives are right. Rather than being in-tent on correction, let your instruction be grounded in affirmation.

The following illustration from *Our Daily Bread* puts the finishing touches on the importance of upholding self-esteem.

Benjamin West was just trying to be a good babysitter for his little sister, Sally. While his mother was out, Benjamin found some bottles of colored ink and proceeded to paint Sally's portrait. By the time Mrs. West returned, ink blots stained the table, chairs and floor. Benjamin's mother surveyed the mess without a word until she saw the picture. Picking it up she exclaimed, "Why, it's Sally!" And she bent down and kissed her son.

In 1763, when Benjamin was twenty-five years old, he was selected as history painter to England's King George III. He became one of the most celebrated artists of his day. Commenting on his start as an artist, he said, "My mother's kiss made me a painter."

Her encouragement did far more than a rebuke would have done. Each of us yearns for someone to fill us, build us and lift us up. We encounter plenty of people along the way intent on letting us know where we've failed, fallen short of expectations, or what areas of our lives are less than perfect. These energy suckers are a dime a dozen. We need people who make us feel valued and worthwhile just as we are.

Remember the basics: *honk encouraging words, believe in people more than they believe in themselves, freely express your love, and uphold people's self-esteem.*

Make it possible for people to say, "I like myself better when I'm with you."

"Do not do unto others as you expect they should do unto you. Their tastes may not be the same."

GEORGE BERNARD SHAW

Encouragement

"Praise is like sunlight to the human spirit:
we cannot flower and grow without it."

JESS LAIR

Offer a Shoulder
to Lean On

> "Few things in the world are more powerful than a positive push. A smile. A word of optimism and hope. A 'you can do it' when things are tough."
>
> —*Richard M. DeVos*

The 1992 Olympics in Barcelona, Spain, provided spectators with a multitude of great moments. Reruns of one track and field event live in my memory.

Britain's Derek Redmond had a lifelong dream of winning a gold medal in the 400-meter race. His chances of achieving that dream increased when the gun sounded to begin the semifinals in Barcelona. Redmond was running a great race, and the finish line was clearly in sight as he rounded the turn in the backstretch. Then disaster struck. A sharp pain shot up the back of his leg. He fell face first onto the track with a torn right hamstring.

Sports Illustrated provided this account of the events that followed:

> *As the medical attendants were approaching, Redmond fought to his feet. "It was animal instinct," he would say later. He set out hopping, in a crazed attempt to finish the race. When he reached the stretch, a large man in a T-shirt came out of the stands, hurled aside a security guard and ran to Redmond, embracing him. It was Jim Redmond, Derek's father. "You don't have to do this," he told his weeping son. "Yes, I do," said Derek. "Well, then," said Jim, "We're going to finish this together."*
>
> *And they did. Fighting off security men, the son's head sometimes buried in his father's shoulder, they stayed in Derek's lane all the way to the end, as the crowd gaped, then rose and howled and wept.*

What a dramatic sight! Derek Redmond failed to capture a gold medal, but he left Barcelona with an incredible memory of a father who left the crowd to share his son's pain. Together, they limped to the finish.

What does this say to us? There isn't a person alive who hasn't experienced the disappointment of unmet expectations. Things don't always go as planned in the pursuit of our dreams. Unexpected obstacles, unplanned events, or the onset of circumstances beyond our control can burst our bubbles. It is amazing how quickly our hopes can vanish followed by the pangs of failure, embarrassment and discouragement.

A word of encouragement during a failure is worth more than a whole load of praise after a success. Orison Swett Marden said, "There is no medicine like hope, no incentive so great, and no tonic so powerful as expectation of something better tomorrow." You can be the distributor of hope that propels someone past the present burden and into future possibilities.

Understanding how quickly momentum can be brought to an abrupt halt increases our sensitivity to how others feel when disappointments sabotage their dreams. It's then that people need someone who cares enough about them to come out of the crowd and onto the track. Let them know you are there for them. Offer a shoulder to lean on to help carry them through the pain. They may not attain the level of success they desired, but they'll never forget the person who lifted them up when they felt let down.

"The worst part of success is trying to find someone who is happy for you."
BETTE MIDLER

Helping People
Believe in Themselves

> "Those who believe in our ability do more than stimulate us. They create for us an atmosphere in which it becomes easier to succeed."
>
> *John H. Spalding*

Yogi Berra was asked whether he thought Don Mattingly's performance in 1984 exceeded his expectations. Yogi responded, "No, but he did a lot better than I thought he would."

Yogi Berra was a master of confusing messages. Yet, our message concerning what we expect of others is normally received loud and clear.

Tommy was having a difficult time in school. He was full of questions and tended to fall behind on class assignments. Tommy's teacher became frustrated with his performance and told his mother that Tommy had little chance for academic achievement or life success.

Tommy's mother believed differently. She removed Tommy from the low-expectation environment and taught him herself. She nurtured his inquisitive nature and encouraged him to use failure as a signal to find another way.

What happened? Tommy became an inventor, recording more than a thousand patents. We can thank him for the lights in our homes and countless other electronic inventions. Thomas Edison thrived on the hope created by his mother's positive expectations.

Our mission in relationships should not be to impress others but to get people to believe in themselves. When we express faith, the door is opened for people to think higher of themselves. That confidence in themselves creates an environment where people feel safe to risk going beyond where they are. Every time you express positive expectations in someone, you are providing life-sustaining nutrition.

Rent the movie *Stand and Deliver*. Watch how calculus teacher Jaime Escalante worked with high school students in East Los Angeles. Keep in mind that was a part of the country where high expectations were virtually non-existent and the idea of quality education was a hopeless pursuit.

Escalante endeavored to work with his students to exceed all previous society-imposed and self-imposed limitations. He was committed to offering them an opportunity to believe in themselves and create hope for the future. His students responded.

I smiled when the Educational Testing Service voiced their skepticism about the results earned by Escalante's students. The ETS investigated the class for cheating. Ultimately, the service provider had to admit that Escalante's students had honorably achieved their scores. This great teacher challenged their minds and instilled belief in themselves.

In order for you to get people to feel important, you must see their value. What I look for in people, I see. What I see, I communicate. What I communicate stimulates people to respond accordingly. What do you see in and expect of others?

"The only person who behaves sensibly is my tailor. He takes my measurements anew every time he sees me, while all the rest go on with their old measurements and expect me to fit them."

GEORGE BERNARD SHAW

"Understanding is a two-way street."

ELEANOR ROOSEVELT

Understanding

Putting Yourself in
Their World

> *"To love you as I love myself is to seek to hear you as I want to be heard and understand you as I long to be understood."*
>
> *David Augsburger*

My daughter became frustrated a few weeks into her freshman year of high school. Normally a happy, vivacious, young lady, she felt overwhelmed by the pressures of school, conflict with friends, teacher expectations, and the time demands of extra-curricular activities. As Katy told me her traumatic experiences, I tried to console her by telling her everything would be okay and that she need not be distressed by these minor difficulties.

"That's easy for you to say, Dad," she responded. "You have all your problems over with."

From a teenager's perspective, adults are all through with their problems and life is one continuous party. Even more important, I think Katy was trying to tell me she could use a little empathy. She wanted me to understand what it feels like to be a freshman. I gave my daughter sound, practical, and realistic advice when all she really wanted was an understanding heart. This could have been a magical father-daughter moment. Instead, it was just another conversation.

Poet Shel Silverstein wrote a heart-touching verse entitled, "The Little Boy and the Old Man." It portrays a young boy talking to an elderly gentleman.

> *Said the little boy, "Sometimes I drop my spoon."*
> *Said the old man, "I do that too."*
> *The little boy whispered, "I wet my pants."*
> *"I do that too," laughed the little old man.*
> *Said the little boy, "I often cry."*
> *The old man nodded, "So do I."*
> *"But worst of all," said the boy, "it seems*
> *Grown-ups don't pay attention to me."*
> *And he felt the warmth of a wrinkled old hand.*
> *"I know what you mean," said the little old man.*

Most people think they see the world as it is. Unfortunately, we really see the world as we are.

I saw my daughter's difficulties through the eyes of a grown-up, not a high school freshman. The little boy saw the world through his eyes, which he learned were much like the eyes of the old man. In a world obsessed with "me" there is a tremendous opportunity to touch people's lives by focusing on what's important to them.

A common obstacle to understanding another person is the limiting belief that his or her world mirrors mine.

I know that doesn't sound too profound, but the significance of that statement is an entryway to people's hearts. To realize that others don't necessarily think like me, act like me, feel like I feel, or respond to every situation as I would respond prepares me to gain valuable insights that might otherwise have been overlooked.

The ability to truly understand other people is a valuable asset. It involves opening your mind and heart with an insatiable desire to help people feel understood. A sincere attempt is made in every conversation to think how others think and feel what others are feeling. If every conversation began and evolved around this intent, I wonder how many conflicts could be avoided.

Are your daily conversations motivated by a desire to get people to understand you, or are you committed in every conversation to put yourself in the other person's world? See their world, experiences, hopes, fears and dreams as they see them. The benefits are immeasurable, because for every person we sincerely seek to understand, there will be someone who wants to do the same for us.

Make it possible for someone today to say,
"When I'm with you, I feel understood."

"Sometimes you can defuse a difficult situation simply by being willing to understand the other person. Often all that people need is to know that someone else cares about how they feel and is attempting to understand their position."

BRIAN TRACY

Could You Just Listen?

> "Most of the successful people I've known are ones who do more listening than talking. If you choose your company carefully, it's worth listening to what they have to say. You don't have to blow out the other fellow's light to let your own shine."
>
> *—Bernard M. Baruch*

It happens about once a week. My wife and I have a nice conversation about a favorite topic, or she will fill me in on the details of an upcoming event. A little while later, I ask a question that she already addressed in our conversation. She then looks at me and says, "You never listen to me." Ouch. I do listen, I think, but for some reason a portion of the information just seems to leak from my memory. Although I think I know how to listen, my actions often prove differently.

John Maxwell tells a delightful story about an eighty-nine-year-old woman with hearing problems who visited her doctor. After examining her, the doctor said, "We now have a procedure that can correct your hearing problem. When would you like to schedule the operation?"

"There won't be any operation because I don't want my hearing corrected," said the woman. "I'm eighty-nine-years-old, and I've heard enough!"

There are times, at any age, when we might think, "I've heard enough, and I don't care to listen anymore." Karl Menninger believes, "The friends who listen to us are the ones we move toward, and we want to sit in their radius." If a relationship is important to us, it is wise to remember that the difference between someone feeling comfortable with us or avoiding us is often our willingness to listen.

The following poem reveals the feelings of someone who badly wants to be heard.

When I ask you to listen to me
and you start giving me advice,
you have not done what I asked.

When I ask you to listen to me
and you tell me I shouldn't feel that way,
you are trampling on my feelings.

When I ask you to listen to me
and you feel you have to do something to solve my problem,
you have failed me, strange as that may seem.

Listen! All I asked was that you listen,
not talk to or do—just hear me.

Advice is cheap—10 cents will get you both Dear Abby
and Billy Graham in the same newspaper.

I can do that for myself; I'm not helpless—,
maybe discouraged and faltering, but not helpless.

When you do something for me that I can and need to do
for myself, you contribute to my fear and weakness.

But, when you accept as a simple fact that I do feel what I feel,
no matter how irrational,
then I can quit trying to convince you

*and can get about the business of understanding what's
behind this irrational feeling.*

*And when that's clear, the answers are obvious
and I don't need advice.
Irrational feelings make sense when we understand.*

*Perhaps that's why prayer works, sometimes, for some
people because God is mute and He doesn't give advice
or try to fix things.
"They" just listen and let you work it out for yourself.*

*So, please listen and just hear me.
And, if you want to talk, wait a minute for your turn—
and I'll listen to you.*

—Anonymous

This unknown writer was expressing a frustration experienced every day by a multitude of people. From the corporate office to the school playground, from the hospital room to the bedroom, and from the subway to the carpool, you will find people who genuinely feel that no one is interested in their lives. Paul Tournier addressed this universal need. "It is impossible," he said, "to overemphasize the immense need humans have to be really listened to, to be taken seriously, to be understood. No one can develop freely in this world and find their life full, without feeling understood by at least one person…Listen to all the conversations of our world, between nations as well as between couples. They are for the most part, dialogues of the deaf."

Studies indicate that we spend 30 percent of a normal business day speaking, 16 percent reading, 9 percent writing, and 45 percent—the majority of our time—listening. Yet, very few people have studied or mastered listening techniques even though close to half of our day is spent in such activity.

An unofficial listening study offers this perspective: "We hear half of what is being said, listen to half of what we hear, understand half of it, believe half of that, and remember only half of that." If you translate those assumptions into an eight-hour work day, it means that:

- *You spend half your day—about four hours—in listening activities.*

- *You hear about two hours' worth of what is said.*

- *You actually listen to an hour of it.*

- *You understand only thirty minutes of that hour.*

- *You believe only fifteen minutes' worth.*

- *And you remember less than eight minutes of all that is said.*

Statistics indicate the importance and difficulty of listening as well as the widespread listening incompetence most people display. The world needs people who aspire to be listeners. Ironically, they not only enhance others' lives but their own as well. It is a win-win affair, and the benefits of acquiring this important skill are enjoyed through-out our lives.

"Listening, like reading, is primarily an activity of the mind, not of the ear or the eye. When the mind is not actively involved in the process, it should be called hearing, not listening..."

MORTIMER ADLER

"Develop an attitude of gratitude, and give thanks
for everything that happens to you,
knowing that every step forward is
a step toward achieving something bigger
and better than your current situation."

BRIAN TRACY

How to phrase it
when you want to
Praise It

> "In spite of our supersonic generation, high-tech wizardry, and computer gadgetry, there is no technical tool equal to praise."
>
> —*Jerry D. Twentier*

Upon accepting an award, Jack Benny once remarked, "I really don't deserve this. But I have arthritis, and I don't deserve that either."

Wouldn't it be great if appreciation would become as natural to give as undesirable life experiences were to contract? How many times do small, seemingly insignificant actions go unnoticed? The doers of such tasks feel they would be better off getting attention in unacceptable ways.

Consider the employee who came in late one morning only to be greeted by his supervisor who says, "Sam, you're late!"

Sam goes about his duties thinking, "So that's what I need to do to get noticed. Day in and day out I do my job without anyone paying any attention. Come in late and finally, they know I'm working here."

People want to believe their efforts deserve praise, and they are willing to go to great lengths to receive it. Yet, expressing appreciation is one of the most neglected acts in relationships. When you observe people doing good things, let them know you recognize it. How? Glad you asked. Here are some simple phrases that will help you praise people and encourage them to repeat their positive behavior:

"I appreciate the way you…"
"I'm impressed with…"
"You're terrific, because…"
"Thanks for going all out when you…"
"One of the things I enjoy most about you is…"
"I admire your …"
"Great job with…"
"I really enjoy working with you because…"
"Our team couldn't be successful without your…"
"Thank you for your…"
"You made my day when…"

"You can be proud of your…"

"You did an outstanding job of…"

"It's evident you have the ability to…"

"I like your…"

"You deserve a pat on the back for …"

"You should be proud of yourself for …"

"I admire the way you take the time to… "

"You're really good at…"

"You've got my support with… "

"What a great idea!"

"It's evident you have a special knack of…"

"You were a great help when…"

"You have a special gift for… "

"I enjoy being with you because you… "

"You're doing a top-notch job of…"

"It's fun watching you…"

"I know you can do it!"

"I believe in you."

"Your commitment to _____ is appreciated!"

The power of positive praise is limited only by its lack of use. How many people do you know who could benefit from a sincere "congratulations" or "great job" or possibly even "you're the best"? Silent appreciation doesn't mean much. Let others know your positive regards toward them. They'll live up to your compliment.

Samuel Goldwyn said, "When someone does something good, applaud! You will make two people happy." Take time to look through that list of phrases you can use to applaud people. Use them frequently. Find additional ways to praise and increase people's good feelings about themselves. You'll be happy you did.

"I believe that you should praise people whenever you can; it causes them to respond as a thirsty plant responds to water."

MARY KAY ASH

Happiness is...
Living Every Moment

> "To experience happiness we must train ourselves
> to live in this moment, to savor it for what it is,
> not running ahead in anticipation of some future date
> nor lagging behind in the paralysis of the past."
>
> *Luci Swindoll*

Dennis Wholey, author of *Are You Happy?*, reported that according to expert opinion, perhaps only 20 percent of Americans are happy. In another national survey, it was estimated that 29 percent of us are happy.

Regardless of the accuracy of these statistics, there is a pretty good indication that people want more in their lives. There is a hole somewhere waiting to be filled and thereby producing happiness. Actually, unhappy people simply have a gap between what they expect and what they are experiencing. That's why happiness has very little to do with what we attain. The more we get, the higher our expectations, and the more likely a larger gap will be created.

Unhappy people would probably agree with the wry definition of happiness offered by psychiatrist Thomas Szasz, who said, "Happiness is an imaginary condition, formerly attributed by the living to the dead, now usually attributed by adults to children, and by children to adults." According to this definition, happiness is anywhere we don't happen to be.

Former child star Shirley Temple Black told a story about her husband, Charles, and his mother. When Charles was a boy, he asked his mother what the happiest moment of her life was.

"This moment—right now," she responded.

"But what about all the other happy moments in your life?" he said, surprised. "What about when you were married?"

"My happiest moment then was then," she answered. "My happiest moment now is now. You can only really live in the moment you're in. So to me, that's always the happiest moment."

I love Mrs. Black's perspective. Whenever you focus on the past, you strip the present of its beauty. And, when you get caught up in the future, you rob the present of its potential.

Happiness seems so simple—and yet, so difficult to define. Norman Cousins, former editor of *Saturday Review*, wrote, "Happiness is probably the easiest emotion to feel, the most elusive to create deliberately, and the most difficult to define. It is experienced differently by different people." I suggest, after considerable thought, that happiness is an existing state of joyful contentment, accompanied by a peace about the present and hope for the future. Happiness is a by-product experienced by looking at all the good and bad in any given moment and then choosing to focus on the good—such an easy concept but a difficult habit to acquire.

"A happy person," said Hugh Downs of ABC's *20/20*, "is not a person in a certain set of circumstances, but rather a person with a certain set of attitudes." Dr. Norman Vincent Peale agrees. "Happiness," he said, "is not a matter of good fortune or worldly possessions. It's a mental attitude. It comes from appreciating what we have, instead of being miserable about what we don't have. It's so simple—yet so hard for the human mind to comprehend."

Here's a little help in developing the attitudes that nurture the seeds of happiness.

1. Accept life's difficulties. I know you know this, but let me remind you that life will never be void of problems. Pain and difficulty are constantly perched at your back door. They are inevitable experiences of living in an imperfect world. A great starting point to happiness is to accept these unpleasant experiences as quickly as you do the joys. To be content in the ups and downs of life epitomizes a truly happy person.

2. Choose happiness now. Waiting for your life to be totally in order before experiencing happiness is an unrealistic dream. "If only…" and "Someday I'll…" are detours to happiness. They snuff out contentment. The best part of your life is right now, not some day in the past or future. Life may not be as good as you want, but you really have it pretty good. Learn to be happy with what you have while you pursue all that you want.

3. Learn to look for the good. Try looking for the positives in your job, relationships, community, church and children. Guard against focusing on the negatives or things that fall short of your expectations. Identify the little things that bring you a sprinkle of happiness. You'll be pleasantly surprised how developing a mindset that looks for the good prepares you to deal more positively with the problems you encounter.

4. **Help others experience happiness.** Bertrand Russell once said, "If there were in the world today any large number of people who desired their own happiness more than they desired the unhappiness of others, we could have a paradise in a few years." Let go of judging. Accept people where they are. Expect the best from others. Help people believe in themselves. Become an inverse paranoid. You read that right. Inverse paranoids are people who think everyone is out to make them happy. Just imagine everyone you meet wanting to bring happiness to your life. And then try to do the same for them.

5. **Decide what you want in life.** In the early 1980s, two Harvard psychologists completed a study of people who called themselves happy. And what did happy people have in common? Money? Success? Power? Health? Love?

None of the above.

Happy people had only two things in common: They knew exactly what they wanted, and they felt they were moving toward getting it.

Dr. Benjamin Spock concurred. He said, "Happiness is mostly a by-product of doing what makes us feel fulfilled." The ultimate in personal happiness is to be actively involved in something bigger than ourselves that causes us to stretch beyond where we are.

On the flip side, unhappiness can be experienced by not knowing what we want and working like crazy to get it. "Many persons have the wrong idea of what constitutes true happiness," advised Helen Keller. "It is not attained through self-gratification but through fidelity to a worthy purpose."

Sometimes I think we work far too hard at trying to be happy. The more we pursue happiness, the more evasive it becomes. As Harold Kushner wrote in the best-selling book *When All You've Ever Wanted Isn't Enough*, "Happiness is a butterfly—the more you chase it, the more it flies away from you and hides. But stop chasing it, put away your net and busy yourself with other, more productive things than the pursuit of happiness, and it will sneak up on you from behind and perch on your shoulder."

If you really want to be happy, the only person that can stop you is you. Don't strive to be happy. Be happy. Wake up each morning.

Smile. Look for the good in the day. Choose to act happy. Find the good in others. Work toward something larger than yourself. Do the best you can in every endeavor.

Be encouraged by Denis Waitley's insight on happiness. "Happiness cannot be traveled to, owned, earned, worn, or consumed. Happiness is the spiritual experience of living every minute with love, grace, and gratitude."

"Just remember, happiness is having a poor memory about what happened yesterday."

LOU HOLTZ

SECTION NINE

"The great gift of
        human beings is that
    we have the power of empathy."

MERYL STREEP

Empathy

Getting Even

> "You will find as you look back upon your life
> that the moments that stand out, the moments
> when you have really lived, are the moments
> when you have done things in a spirit of love."
>
> *Henry Drummond*

During the days of the Berlin Wall, a few East Berliners decided to send their West Berlin neighbors a "gift." They proceeded to load a dump truck with undesirables, including garbage, broken bricks, building material, and any other disgusting items they could find. They calmly drove across the border, received clearance, and delivered their present by dumping it on the West Berlin side.

Needless to say, the West Berliners were irritated and intent on "getting even." People immediately began offering ideas on how to out-do the repulsive actions of their adversaries. A wise man interrupted their angry reactions and offered an entirely different approach. Surprisingly, people responded favorably to his suggestions and began loading a dump truck full of essential items that were scarce in East Berlin. Clothes, food and medical supplies poured in. They drove the loaded truck across the border, carefully unloaded and stacked the precious commodities, then left a sign that read, "Each gives according to his ability to give."

Imagine the reaction of those who saw the "payback" and powerful message on the sign. Shock. Embarrassment. Distrust. Unbelief. Maybe even a bit of regret.

What we give to others sends a loud message about who we are. How we respond to unkindness, unfairness, or ingratitude reveals our true character.

"Shall we make a new rule of life from tonight: always to try to be a little kinder than is necessary."

JAMES M. BARRIE

Never Assume
You're Pedaling Together

> "We are born for cooperation, as are the feet,
> the hands, the eyelids and the upper and lower jaws.
> People need each other to make up for
> what each one does not have."
>
> —*Marcus Aurelius*

The definition of the word cooperation stems from two Latin words, co, meaning "with," and opus, meaning "work." So, quite literally, cooperation means working with others. Sounds simple, doesn't it?

For over twenty-five years the *Des Moines Register* newspaper has sponsored a summer Register's Annual Great Bike Ride Across Iowa (RAGBRAI). Bikers from all over the country emerge on the western side of Iowa, determined to be one of hundreds of successful riders who invest a week pedaling their way across the state.

One year, RAGBRAI designated our community as a stopping point for the night. It was an incredible sight to watch the bikers swarm into town and set up camp. Young and old alike enjoyed the challenge, fellowship, and fun that accompanied this popular event.

As I walked through one of the camping areas, I overheard a conversation between two riders who were navigating the trail together on a tandem bike. The man was complaining about the difficulty of one of the hills they had to climb earlier in the day. "That was a struggle," he said. "I thought for sure we were going to have to push the bike up the hill on foot."

"It sure was a steep hill," his female companion responded, "and if I hadn't kept the brake on all the way, we would have rolled back down for sure."

There's practically no limit to what people can accomplish when they work cooperatively. However, if just one person drags his feet or continually applies the brake, everyone else suffers. Married couples, departments at work, athletic teams, bands, boards, dancers, or the cast in a play need to understand where the team is going, how they will get there, and what effort will be required by each person.

When riding a bike together, remember to peddle together. Work with a spirit of cooperation.

"The purpose of life is to collaborate for a common cause; the problem is nobody seems to know what it is."

GERHARD GSCHWANDTNER

"Three grand essentials to happiness in this life are something to do, something to love, and something to hope for."

JOSEPH ADDISON

Hope

How Do
People Feel
Around You?

> "People love others not for who they
> are but for how they make us feel."
>
> —*Irwin Federman*

I wish you could meet my daughter. Katy is a vibrant, enthusiastic, young lady with a fabulous approach toward life. As a fourth grader, she committed herself to an enviable work ethic, developed a magnetic personality, and endeared the respect of her teacher. (Of course, I'm entirely objective about my assessment.)

At the end of Katy's first semester as a fourth grader, a parent-teacher conference was scheduled for Thursday afternoon at 4:30 p.m. She was especially excitable during the week and confirmed the meeting time with her mother and me on several occasions. We assured her that both of us planned to attend this special event.

On Wednesday morning, Katy approached her teacher before school started. "I sure wish my conference was today!" she exclaimed.

"Isn't tomorrow a good day for your parents to come?" her insightful teacher, Mrs. DeJong, queried.

"Oh no, they'll both be here," Katy responded, "I just wish my conference was today."

Fascinated by this unusual student attitude, Mrs. DeJong probed further. "Why would you like me to meet with your parents today, Katy?"

Katy flashed one of her heartwarming smiles as she blurted, "I just can't wait for them to come home and tell me how good I am!"

Being a good student, Katy knew the parent-teacher conference was one avenue for her to receive a bit of recognition. She also knew that my wife and I made it a habit to discuss the conference with the kids. It didn't take a rocket scientist to see why Katy was anxious for her conference. This was her opportunity to hear how good she was, even though she already knew.

My wife and I have ample reason to support and encourage our children. They are good kids. I'm concerned that I spend far too little time looking for ways to encourage and an excessive amount of time searching for things to correct. It's amazing how conditioned I've become—conditioned to believe a parent's role is to correct, discipline and direct. I'm fine with that when balanced with support, recognition and encouragement. Oh, to find that perfect balance.

Encouragers do what? Build our hopes. Support our dreams. Understand our difficulties. Recognize our efforts. Celebrate with us in our achievements. Keep us from going to bed with an aching stomach, broken heart or damaged spirit. They know what to say and when to say it. Encouragers provide nourishment for the soul.

Become an encourager. Make it possible for people to say, "I like myself better when I'm with you."

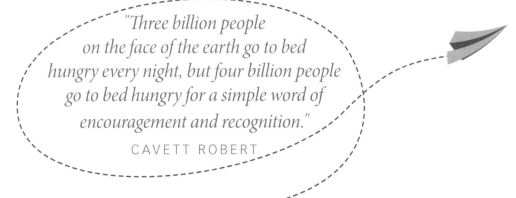

"Three billion people on the face of the earth go to bed hungry every night, but four billion people go to bed hungry for a simple word of encouragement and recognition."

CAVETT ROBERT

Give Yourself Away

> "Only those who have learned the power of sincere and selfless contribution experience life's deepest joy: true fulfillment."
>
> *Anthony Robbins*

There are two seas in the Holy Land. The famous Sea of Galilee takes in fresh water from a nearby brook, uses it to generate a variety of marine vegetation, and then passes it on to the Jordan River. The Jordan does its part by spreading the life throughout the desert, turning it into fertile land.

The Dead Sea, on the other hand, comes by its name for a reason—it's dead. The water in the Dead Sea is so full of salt that no life can exist. The major difference between these two bodies of water is that the Dead Sea takes in the water from the Jordan River and hangs on to it. It has no outlet.

What a perfect example of the differences in people. People who live without giving themselves away become stagnant. What they keep stifles them. Those who freely give of themselves multiply life. Eric Butterworth said, "A committed giver is an incurably happy person, a secure person, a satisfied person and a prosperous person."

There's a life-enhancing lesson here. If you don't sow anything today, you'll have nothing to reap in the future. A rich life is the direct result of enriching others. "Don't judge each day by the harvest you reap," advised Robert Louis Stevenson, "but by the seeds that you plant."

According to the *New York Times*, Mr. Milton Petrie enjoyed giving his money away. Petrie, the son of a Russian immigrant pawn shop owner, researched New York papers "for stories of people life had kicked in the face. He then reached for his checkbook."

Petrie built his fortune with a chain of women's clothing stores. His lifelong commitment to generous giving continued even after he died at age ninety-two. The newspaper headline reporting his death said: "Millionaire's Death Doesn't Stop His Generosity." His will reportedly named 451 beneficiaries of his $800 million estate.

"What keeps our interest in life and makes us look forward to tomorrow is giving pleasure to other people," advised Eleanor Roosevelt. "Happiness is not a goal, it is a by-product."

Did you know that Elvis Presley never took a tax deduction for his donations to charities, believing it violated the spirit of giving?

General William Booth had a passion for the poor of London and committed himself to a mission of meeting those needs. By the time of his death, Booth's local mission had spread across the world. His final sermon, delivered from a hospital bed to an international convention of Salvation Army "soldiers," was simply a one-word telegram that read: "Others!"

Booth's one-word sermon encapsulated everything he believed about the purpose of living—giving unselfishly of yourself to benefit others.

Billionaire John D. Rockefeller, Sr. lived the first part of his life as a miserable man, unable to sleep, feeling unloved, and surrounded by bodyguards. At age fifty-three, he was diagnosed with a rare disease. He lost all of his hair, and his body became shrunken. Medical experts gave him a year to live.

Rockefeller started thinking beyond his current life and sought meaning to his existence. He gave away his money to churches and the poor, and he established the Rockefeller Foundation. His life turned around, his health improved and, contrary to the doctor's prediction, he lived to be ninety-eight.

John D. Rockefeller's life exemplified the transformation that's possible when the joy of giving is discovered. You might be tempted to think that if you had Rockefeller's wealth, giving to others would be easy. Although it's easy to find examples of people with wealth who gave it away, what we're talking about here is much more than writing a check to your favorite charity. That's only a tiny portion of the message.

"Every person passing through life will unknowingly leave something and take something away," reflected Robert Fulghum. "Most of this 'something' cannot be seen or heard or numbered or scientifically detected or counted…The census doesn't count it. Nothing counts without it."

People like John Wesley make Fulghum's "something" a way of life. Wesley said, "Do all the good you can, in all the ways you can, to all the souls you can, in every place you can, at all the times you can, with all the zeal you can, as long as ever you can."

You can keep the waters of life flowing and add tremendous value by giving yourself to others. Put others first in your thinking. Find ways to enrich their lives. Give unselfishly. It is a natural law of life that the more of yourself that you pass on to others with no expectation of receiving in return, the more your life will be blessed.

If you want to experience ongoing success, learn to give yourself away. "Success is not rare. It is common," believed Henry Ford, Sr. "It is not a matter of luck or of contesting, for certainly no success can come from preventing the success of another. It is a matter of adjusting one's efforts to overcome obstacles and one's abilities to give the services needed by others. There is no other possible success. Most people think of it in terms of getting; success, however, begins in terms of giving."

"Lock your house, go across the railroad tracks, find someone in need, and do something to help that person."

~ DR. KARL MENNINGER

About the Author

Glenn Van Ekeren is the President for Vetter Health Services in Omaha, Nebraska—a company specializing in quality care and services that are changing the view of long-term care for our senior citizens. For the past forty years, Glenn's primary profession has been helping people grow. His passion as a leader is to create a work environment where people feel good about themselves, their jobs, the people they work with, the people they serve and their organizations.

As a professional speaker, he is known for his inspiring, enthusiastic, and down-to-earth approach for maximizing people and organizational potential. Glenn has also traveled the country providing more than 1,000 seminars and keynote addresses to over 100,000 people.

Glenn is the author of the popular *12 Simple Secrets of Happiness* series including:

12 Simple Secrets to Finding Fulfillment at Work

12 Simple Secrets to Staying Calm in a Crazy World

12 Simple Secrets to Experiencing Joy in Everyday Relationships

In addition, he penned:

The Speaker's Sourcebook

The Speakers Sourcebook II

His popular inspirational blog can be enjoyed at
www.enthusedaboutlife.com

Glenn is also a featured author in many of the early *Chicken Soup for the Soul* books, and the editor for Braude's *Treasury of Wit & Humor* and *The Complete Speaker's & Toastmaster's Library*. His works have been translated and published in 19 foreign countries.

Glenn's motto in life is "to live every moment of every day to the fullest." His practical power-packed messages capture people's attention, stir emotions, motivate people to stretch toward their potential and provide practical strategies for personal and organizational growth.